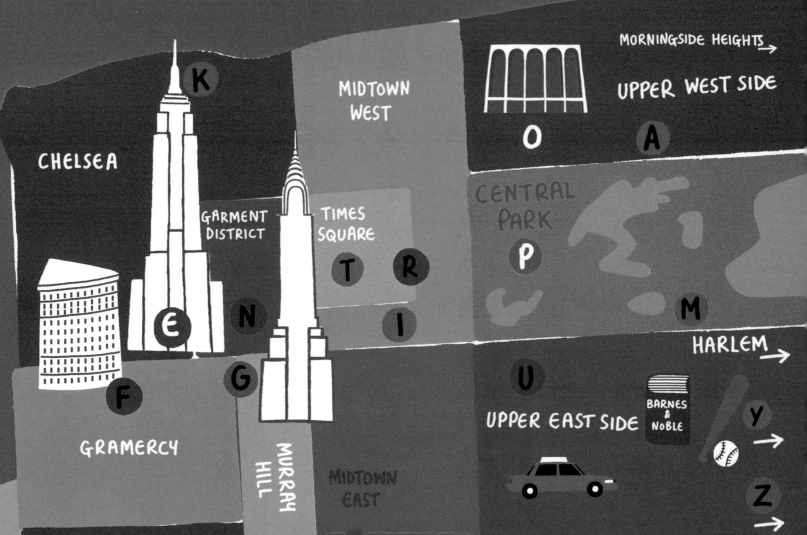

MORNINGSIDE HEIGHTS →

UPPER WEST SIDE

MIDTOWN WEST

CHELSEA

K

GARMENT DISTRICT

TIMES SQUARE

CENTRAL PARK

P

T

R

E

N

I

M

HARLEM →

U

H

F

G

GRAMERCY

MURRAY HILL

MIDTOWN EAST

UPPER EAST SIDE

BARNES & NOBLE

Y →

STUYVESANT TOWN

Z →

Q

QUEENS

A	AMERICAN MUSEUM OF NATURAL HISTORY		M	METROPOLITAN MUSEUM OF ART
B	BROOKLYN BRIDGE		N	NEW YORK PUBLIC LIBRARY
C	CONEY ISLAND		O	OPERA
D	DOWNTOWN		P	CENTRAL PARK
E	EMPIRE STATE BUILDING		Q	QUEENS
F	FLATIRON BUILDING		R	RADIO CITY MUSIC HALL
G	GRAND CENTRAL TERMINAL		S	SUBWAY
H	HIGH LINE		T	TIMES SQUARE
I	ICE SKATING		U	UPTOWN
J	JFK AIRPORT		V	GREENWICH VILLAGE
K	KING KONG		W	WATER TOWERS
L	LADY LIBERTY		X	STOCK EXCHANGE
			Y	YANKEE STADIUM
			Z	BRONX ZOO

For my mum and for Marie-Louise

Mixed media and digital techniques were used to create the full-color art.

Published by Sourcebooks, Inc.
P.O. Box 4410, Naperville, Illinois 60567-4410
(630) 961-3900
Fax: (630) 961-2168
sourcebooks.com

Originally published in 2016 in Great Britain by Hodder Children's Books, an imprint of Hodder and Stoughton.

Library of Congress Cataloging-in-Publication Data is on file with the publisher.

Source of Production: Wing King Tong Limited, Hong Kong
Date of Production: July 2017
Run Number: 5009862

Printed and bound in China
10 9 8 7 6 5 4 3 2 1

NY IS FOR NEW YORK

PAUL THURLBY

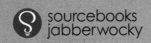

sourcebooks
jabberwocky

THE AMERICAN MUSEUM OF NATURAL HISTORY

is one of the largest museums in the world. It contains over 32 million specimens, including plants, animals, and fossils.

Its collections include diverse dioramas, ancient artifacts, and precious stones.

AMERICAN
MUSEUM OF NATURAL HISTORY

It was the first steel-wire suspension bridge constructed.

is one of the oldest major bridges in the United States. Completed in 1883, it spans the East River to connect the boroughs of Manhattan and Brooklyn.

Coney Island is the original amusement destination in New York. Crowds of sun-seekers head to the beach on a summer's day.

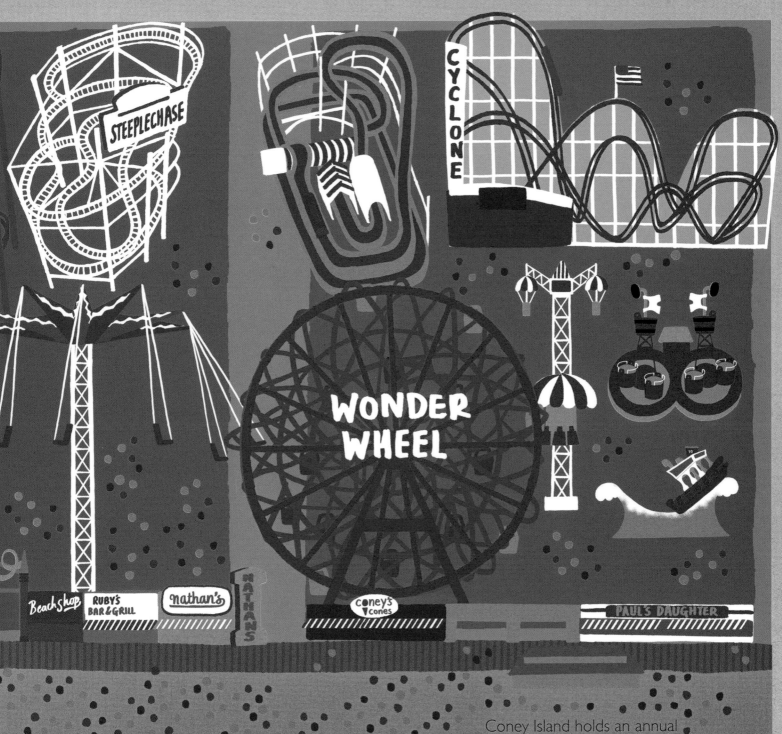

Coney Island holds an annual hot dog-eating contest.

DOWNTOWN MANHATTAN

has a diverse community and a vibrant nightlife, and it attracts many artists and musicians.

Downtown neighborhoods include Tribeca, Chinatown, and Little Italy.

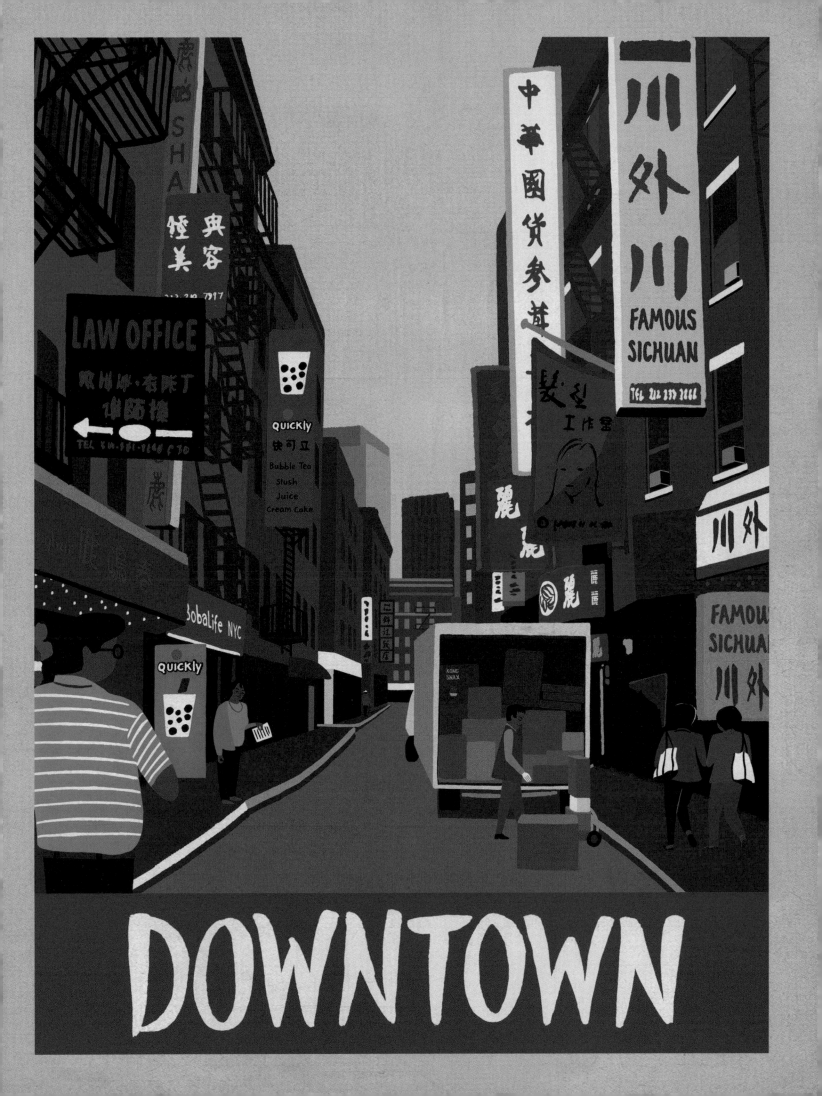

THE Empire STATE BUILDING

is a 103-story skyscraper and stands at a total of 1,454 feet high.

Opened on May 1, 1931, the whole structure was built in just 410 days.

It has 1,860 steps and 73 elevators!

EMPIRE STATE BUILDING

THE FLATIRON BUILDING

is one of New York's oldest skyscrapers. It has 22 floors and is as skinny as it looks. It derives its name from its resemblance to a clothes iron.

The Strand Bookstore, south of the Flatiron district, is home to 18 miles of new, used, and rare books.

FLATIRON

GRAND CENTRAL TERMINAL

is one of the largest railroad stations in the world. It has 44 platforms and 67 tracks, more tracks than any other railroad station.

The Chrysler Building is across the block from Grand Central Terminal. It is considered one of the most beautiful pieces of art deco architecture in Manhattan.

The Grand Central clock is New York's most famous timepiece.

GRAND CENTRAL
TERMINAL

The High Line is a 1.45-mile-long park built on a disused railway track. This cool promenade has been redesigned and is now surrounded by trees and plants. It allows visitors to take a traffic-free walk above the busy streets below.

The park gets nearly five million visitors annually.

HIGH LINE

Rockefeller Center in winter is a popular attraction. Visitors lace up their skates and swirl away at The Rink among bustling crowds, sparkling lights, and a unique urban backdrop.

The Rockefeller Center Christmas Tree Lighting is a favorite annual event in New York City.

JFK AIRPORT

is one of the busiest international airports in the United States. It is home to six passenger terminals, four runways, and over ninety airlines!

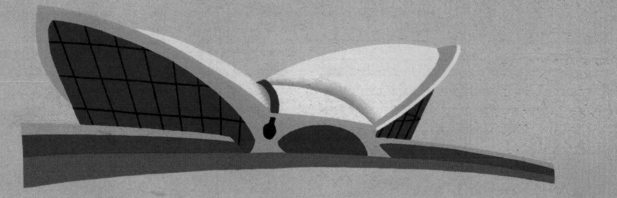

JFK was originally known as Idlewild Airport, even after two successive name changes, before being officially renamed John F. Kennedy International Airport in 1963.

JFK AIRPORT

KING KONG

is a landmark black-and-white film about a gigantic gorilla called "Kong." In a memorable and terrifying scene, he escapes his captors and climbs up the Empire State Building only to fall dramatically to the streets below.

Ann Darrow is the fictional character with whom the giant ape falls in love. She is played by Fay Wray in the original 1933 movie.

THE STATUE OF LIBERTY

is a 305-foot-high copper landmark situated on an island in New York Harbor. Built by the same engineer as the Eiffel Tower, it was a gift to the people of the United States from the people of France in 1886.

The statue's crown has seven rays because the world has seven seas and seven continents.

THE METROPOLITAN MUSEUM OF ART

(also known as The Met) is the largest art museum in the United States, and is among the largest and most visited art museums in the world.

The Little Fourteen-Year-Old Dancer is a sculpture by Edgar Degas of a young student of the Paris Opera Ballet.

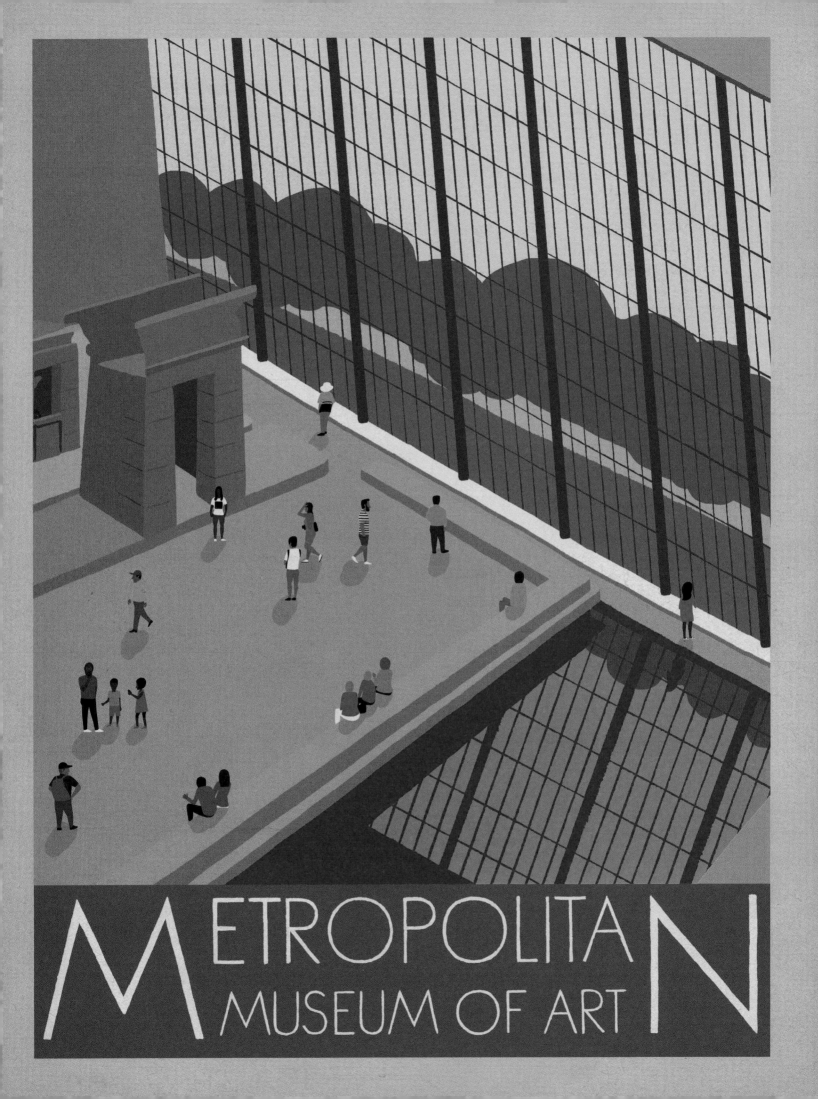

THE NEW YORK PUBLIC LIBRARY

opened in 1911 with a collection of over one million books. Its collections now exceed 50 million items, including not only books but also photographs, films, paintings, musical scores, and sound recordings.

A famous scene in the film *Breakfast at Tiffany's*, starring Audrey Hepburn, featured the library.

NEW YORK
PUBLIC LIBRARY

THE
METROPOLITAN OPERA

has nearly 4,000 seats and is the largest purpose-built opera house in the world. Its innovative program of new and classic productions has helped keep it alive for more than 100 years.

Originally housed at a smaller 39th street venue, the state-of-the-art
Metropolitan Opera House opened in 1966.

More than 750 acres of land were initially set aside for the park, which now covers 843 acres.

Central Park is the most visited urban park in the United States. It hosts year-round activities on its vast lawns, and encompasses many gardens, lakes, and woodlands as well as its own zoo, carousel, and castle.

QUEENS

is the largest in area of the five boroughs of New York City. One of its attractions is Flushing Meadows, home of the New York Mets baseball team and the U.S. Open tennis Grand Slam.

Serena Williams and her sister,
Venus Williams, are regarded by many as two of
the best professional tennis players of all time.

QUEENS

RADIO CITY MUSIC HALL

is an entertainment venue that hosts concerts, stage shows, and film premieres. The art deco music hall opened to the public in 1932 and has 6,000 seats for spectators.

The Great Stage's proscenium arch measures 60 feet high and 100 feet wide, and the gold stage curtain is the largest in the world.

The all-time ridership record is 2.1 billion passengers, set in 1946.

The subway is an essential part of city living in the Big Apple. There are 660 miles of track in use for passenger service, with a further 186 miles of track used for storage and transit.

Approximately 300,000 people walk through Times Square daily.

Times Square is one of the world's most visited tourist attractions, drawing an estimated fifty million visitors annually. It is filled with billboards and is the hub of the Broadway Theatre district.

The Guggenheim is one of the most controversial pieces of architecture ever erected in New York and one of the most awe-inspiring.

Upper Manhattan includes some of the city's most iconic locations such as Central Park and the Solomon R. Guggenheim Museum.

Most streets in Manhattan are known by their numbers, but the streets in Greenwich Village carry names as well.

is often referred to by locals as simply "the Village." It has retained much of its charm and historic character over the years. It is an artists' haven and has some of the best cafés in New York.

WATER TOWERS

are dotted along the skyline in New York.
They may look like relics from a bygone era,
but most New Yorkers still drink and bathe
using the water stored in them.

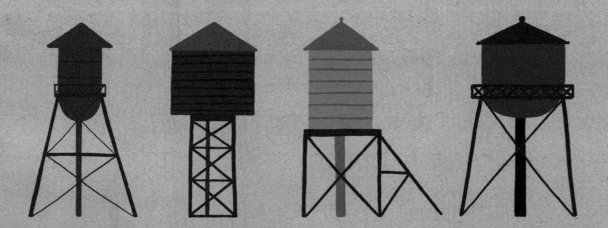

Most buildings in the city taller than six stories need some sort of
water tower to provide water pressure to the buildings' residents.

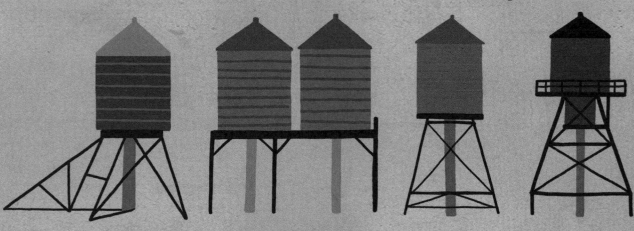

WATER TOWERS

THE NEW YORK STOCK EXCHANGE

is at the heart of America's financial industry. Trading opens at 9:30 a.m. every morning when the opening bell is rung. The closing bell is rung at 4 p.m. to mark the end of trading.

Nelson Mandela, Mr. Potato Head, and Spider-Man have all rung the opening bell.

YANKEE STADIUM

is the home of the New York Yankees baseball team. The fans are some of the loudest and most knowledgeable you will find anywhere.

The new Yankee Stadium opened in 2009. Besides baseball games, Yankee Stadium hosts soccer matches and concerts.

THE BRONX ZOO

is among the largest metropolitan
zoos in the world, with some 6,000
animals, representing more than 600
species from around the globe.

The zoo includes 265 acres of parkland, through which the Bronx River flows.

In September 2015, I first visited New York. Just like that trip, making this book has been a great adventure. For me, using the alphabet is simply a way of structuring the book. From there, I expand on each image and tell the reader more about The Big Apple, taking in some of New York's most famous landmarks and streets.

When in New York, I visited the Empire State Building twice, once at night and once early in morning. It's a special place because a movie star gorilla once climbed up to the top of the building! Can you spot a gorilla on every spread?

Originally from Nottingham, now based in London, I have been a full-time illustrator since September 2006.

I'd like to thank my primary school teachers for seeing that I could draw and write well, despite holding my pen differently, and for recognizing that there is no set way of doing things.

I've built up a large list of commissions working in advertising, design, publishing, and editorial for clients including *The New Yorker,* BBH New York, Mother London, The French Tourist Board, Penguin USA, Ted Baker, Warner/Chappell Music, *The Washington Post,* Pimm's, Sarson's, and The Southbank Centre, London.

Winning the Bologna Ragazzi Opera Prima Award in 2013 for my first book, *Paul Thurlby's Alphabet,* was one of the proudest achievements of my career so far.